WRITING HOME

Alan Bennett first appeared on the stage in 1960 as one of the authors and performers of the revue *Beyond the Fringe*. His stage plays include *Forty Years On*, *Getting On*, *Habeas Corpus*, *The Old Country*, *Enjoy* and *Kafka's Dick*, and he has written many television plays, notably *A Day Out*, *Sunset Across the Bay*, *A Woman of No Importance* and the series of monologues *Talking Heads*. An adaptation of his television play *An Englishman Abroad* was paired with *A Question of Attribution* in the double bill *Single Spies*, first produced at the National Theatre in 1988. This was followed in 1990 by his adaptation of *The Wind in the Willows* and in 1991 by *The Madness of George III*, both produced at the National Theatre. His stage version of *The Lady in the Van* was seen in the West End in 1999. His most recent play, *The History Boys*, premiered at the National Theatre in 2004 and won the *Evening Standard* and Critics' Circle awards for Best Play, the Laurence Olivier Award for Best New Play, and The South Bank Award. His latest collection of prose, *Untold Stories*, is published by Faber and Faber and Profile Books.

Writing Home

ALAN BENNETT

faber and faber

First published in 1994
by Faber and Faber Limited
3 Queen Square London WC1N 3AU
Revised edition first published in 1997
This paperback edition published in 2006

Photoset by Parker Typesetting Service, Leicester
Printed and bound in Great Britain by Mackays of Chatham PLC,
Chatham, Kent

A CIP record for this book
is available from the British Library

ISBN 978-0-571-23241-3
ISBN 0-571-23241-8

2 4 6 8 10 9 7 5 3

Contents

List of Illustrations

The drawing on page 84 showing the removal of Miss Shepherd's van is by David Gentleman.

Introduction

In a Manner of Speaking

This book brings together the talks, diaries and occasional journalism that I have written over the last twenty years or so, mostly for the BBC or the *London Review of Books*. I have called the book *Writing Home*, though there is plenty here that has nothing to do with home and some of it, looked back on, that seems not to have much to do with me.

Most of the journalism was grudgingly undertaken, in particular the book reviews, which were teased out of me (in both senses) by my friend Mary-Kay Wilmers, the present editor of the *London Review of Books*. There are writers, I'm told, who dash off these occasional pieces with ease and pleasure before turning back, reinvigorated, to the job in hand. Not me, I'm afraid. Book reviewing is not my element, demanding a breadth of reading and reference that I generally do not have and which writing plays seldom requires; the result is I find myself either covering up or showing off, while at the same time opting to write in what I imagine to be a metropolitan mode.

That I should admit to having a choice in the way I write isn't an advertisement for versatility so much as an anxiety about sincerity, and it takes me back to a not quite primal scene of my youth.

I was born and brought up in Leeds, where my father was a butcher. As a boy, I sometimes went out on the bike delivering orders to customers, one of whom was a Mrs Fletcher. Mrs

Fletcher had a daughter, Valerie, who went away to school then to London, where she got a job with a publishing firm. She did well in the firm, becoming assistant to one of the directors, whom, though he was much older than she was, she eventually married. The firm was Faber and Faber, and the director was T. S. Eliot. So there was a time when I thought my only connection with the literary world would be that I had once delivered meat to T. S. Eliot's mother-in-law.

A few years later, when my dad had sold the shop but we were still living in Leeds, my mother came in one day and said, 'I ran into Mrs Fletcher down the road. She wasn't with Mr Fletcher; she was with another feller – tall, elderly, very refined-looking. She introduced me, and we passed the time of day.' And it wasn't until some time later that I realized that, without it being one of the most momentous encounters in western literature, my mother had met T. S. Eliot. I tried to explain to her the significance of the great poet, but without much success, *The Waste Land* not figuring very largely in Mam's scheme of things.

'The thing is,' I said finally, 'he won the Nobel Prize.'

'Well,' she said, with that unerring grasp of inessentials which is the prerogative of mothers, 'I'm not surprised. It was a beautiful overcoat.'

I can imagine that meeting: Mam smiling desperately, as she and Dad always did when they were out of their depth; nodding a good deal, too, so as not to have to speak; and, if she has to contribute, trying to 'speak properly', though without 'putting it on' – 'putting it on' being one of the (several) charges Dad had against my mother's sisters, Auntie Kathleen and Auntie Myra, both of whom nursed pretensions to refinement and who never knew, in Dad's words, 'when to keep their traps shut'. It would have taken more than T. S. Eliot to silence them.

Having said goodbye to Mrs Fletcher and the refined gentleman (whoever he was), Mam would have come away wishing she 'had a bit more off' – i.e. more confidence – and regretting that she and Dad hadn't been educated, believing as they always did that education was a passport to social ease and that had they been able to 'stop on at school' everything would have been different.

It wouldn't, of course: it was class and temperament, not want of education, that held their tongues; 'stopping on at school' might have loosened them a little but it never entirely loosened mine, and I stopped on at school one way or another until I was twenty-eight. Thirty years on, this book still shows traces of speech difficulties they passed on to me. What am I doing in book reviews, for instance, but trying to 'speak properly'? What is writing sketches if not 'putting it on'? 'Just be yourself,' my parents would say, ignoring the fact that this was something they themselves seldom managed to be, at any rate in company. Funny and voluble on their own, the slightest social pressure sent them into smiling, nodding silence. But it was different for me, they thought. I was educated; I could be myself; I had a self it was not embarrassing to be.

So I see this awkward encounter with Mr Eliot as a kind of parable, a prefiguring of how, when I did eventually start to write, it should be in two different voices, metropolitan ('speaking properly') and provincial ('being yourself'), and that if one takes T. S. Eliot to represent Art, Culture and Literature (all of them very much in the upper case) and my mother to represent life (resolutely in the lower case), then what happened at the end of Shire Oak Street that morning nearly forty years ago went on happening when I started to write plays and is still happening between the covers of this book.

It wasn't that I had any particular affection for the works of T. S. Eliot. I had seen, though not entirely understood, *The Cocktail Party* when it came to the Leeds Grand Theatre on its provincial tour, and also *Murder in the Cathedral* done at a local church. I had even read *Notes Towards a Definition of Culture*, but only because I was soon to try for a Cambridge scholarship and it seemed the kind of thing one was expected to read. And just as one read what one was expected to read, so, when I started very haltingly to write, I wrote what one was expected to write: not, that is, about life, in my case the life of a northern town – provincial, dull and at that time, the late 1950s, largely unwritten about – but the life that I had read about in books or seen at Saturday matinées at the Grand Theatre – metropolitan, literary and middle-class. Admittedly these first efforts only took the form of sketches and parodies which I performed at concerts in my college at Oxford, but they led in 1960 to my collaboration in the revue *Beyond the Fringe*.

Whether *Beyond the Fringe* was satire was much debated at the time. It scarcely mattered, as there was no debate about how funny it was, though I had a sneaking feeling that some of my contributions were less so and more earnest than the rest. After a spell in the West End the show went to America in 1962, where, despite opening in New York during the week of the Cuban Missile Crisis, it was a great success. Towards the end of 1963 it was decided to revamp it, and, with the addition of some new sketches, the show went into a second edition. It was perhaps the earnestness coming out, and also because I had been away from home for more than a year, that made me decide for the first time to try to speak and write in a voice that was my own, rather than putting one on. I was going to be myself.

What I chose to do was a monologue about death, and in particular death and its supposedly comic aspects in the North of England. Now in 1963 death was not the subject of lively interest it has since become, and even today it's hardly big on Broadway. This was also death as met with in Morecambe and Blackpool, neither of them settings which an American audience could be expected to know about or want to. I performed the sketch nightly for six months to the embarrassment of my colleagues and the stunned silence of the audience, and when the revue ended it was nearly ten years before I ventured to write about the North of England again. So much for 'being myself'. The first round had gone to T. S. Eliot.

And he won the second round too, because when I wrote my first stage play, *Forty Years On* (1968), it had much more to do with art than life, wasn't life at all in fact but the product (and it's not to disparage it to say it's also the waste product) of years of reading memoirs of literary life, tales of novelists' schooldays and the period between the wars. Or, as a character in a later play puts it, somewhat over-elaborately, as he describes a bookshelf:

Horizon, the parish magazine, *Scrutiny*, the school chronicle, all the nice distinctions, careful cross-bearings and distances on the pedometer. Relief maps of anxiety, the contours of small depressions. Get Well cards and invites to funerals. Notes under the general heading of amelioration. Deaths in vicarages and (Little) Venice. Bottles of Jordan water and basinfuls of the warm South. School and the trenches, good talk and good wine and the never-ending siege of the country house. Messages from an unvisited island.

(*The Old Country*)

Set in a public school, part play and part revue, *Forty Years On* had nothing to do with any world that I'd known outside books, let alone with 'being myself'. An elegy for the passing of a traditional England, the play is constructed round a series of literary parodies, which in retrospect I can see were a form of apprenticeship, as indeed had been some of the sketches in *Beyond the Fringe*. Art comes out of art; it begins with imitation, often in the form of parody, and it's in the process of imitating the voices of others that one comes to learn the sound of one's own. This is the theory anyway. With me it hasn't quite worked out like that, the fissure between provincial and metropolitan persisting, T. S. Eliot and my mother shaking but never joining hands.

For a while after *Forty Years On* I kept the voice I had acquired for the stage and the voice I had been born with for television; my first TV plays, *A Day Out* (1972) and *Sunset Across the Bay* (1974), were both set in the North, as have been many others since. This neat division didn't persist all that long, but though I've written several TV plays 'speaking properly' (e.g. *An Englishman Abroad* and *102 Boulevard Haussmann*) I've still only managed one Northern play for the stage (*Enjoy*) and that was hardly a success, as mystifying to a West End audience as the northern way of death had been on Broadway. Sometimes I envy the power of my contemporary, the poet Tony Harrison, who has one defiant Leeds voice to which he subjugates everything he writes. But he had to suffer for his voice at school as I never did, and so sets more store by it (nor, I imagine, did his mother ever meet T. S. Eliot). Not that having two voices is much of a problem, more a worry about consistency – and even that seldom surfaces nowadays, except on occasions like this when I try to make sense of what I have written.

It could all, I suppose, be less ponderously put in terms of wearing this hat or that, except that hats are supposed to give you confidence, not make you uneasy. Speaking is more of a trial than writing, particularly speaking on the radio, and several of the pieces printed here began as radio talks. I tried to lose my northern accent at one period, then reacquired it, and now don't know where I am, sometimes saying my 'a's long, sometimes short, and 'u's a continuing threat, words like 'butcher' and names like 'Cutbush' always lying in ambush. Anyone who ventures south of the Trent is likely to contract an incurable disease of the vowels; it's a disease to which for some reason weather forecasters are particularly prone, and lecturers in sociology.

Some of these pieces have been hard to classify. *Dinner at Noon* is as much reminiscence as it is record, so that puts it among the recollections. I'm sure the address to the Prayer Book Society belongs under 'Books', but what does one call 'Tit for Tatti' or 'Going Round'? Skits, I suppose, though I don't like the word; humour, though I don't like that very much either – too close to the BBC's 'light-hearted look at'. These are the pieces I'm most unsure about and the ones most likely to have dated but for completeness's sake I've included them under 'Stocking Fillers', just glad that I don't feel tempted to write like that any more. I know there are repetitions, but I've made no attempt to eradicate them lest I be left with a literary doily. I think it was Kenneth (not the Chancellor of the Exchequer) Clark who said that most of us have only a few pennies to rattle about in our tins (though he had more, in every sense, than most).

I would like to thank Jean McNicol of the *London Review of Books*, who has edited much of this material. As I've said, many of the pieces would not have been written but for the persistence of Mary-Kay Wilmers and the staff of the *London Review*. The LRB has been in existence now for fifteen years, and it seems to me (and not just because I occasionally contribute to it) the liveliest, most serious and also the most radical literary periodical we have. I would have liked the LRB to have published this volume, as it did the original version of *The Lady in the Van*. That proved not to be possible, but I hope this book will at least bring the paper to the notice of a wider readership.

This revised edition of *Writing Home* includes some additional material: extracts from my diaries for 1993, 1994 and 1995 and some previously overlooked entries from 1986, all again from the *London Review of Books*; there is also an account of the making of the film *The Madness of King George* and two memorial addresses, one delivered at the dedication of a window to A. E. Housman in Westminster Abbey, the other at a service for Peter Cook in Hampstead Parish Church. This latter address was done from what the *Dictionary of National Biography* always refers to as 'personal knowledge'; the Housman piece was not done from personal knowledge at all, though the presentation of the window fell to Enoch Powell, who did know Housman, having been his pupil, and who confirmed that the poet's small talk was largely confined to food.

I note in the new diary material a continuation of that mild depression which has persisted for over sixteen years now, coterminous with the life of a seedy and increasingly discredited administration. In a previously unpublished entry for 11 May 1986 I mention a local doctor in Settle whose prompt action at the time of Chernobyl probably safeguarded the future health of the children of the neighbourhood. Unlike mid-Wales and Cumbria, our area of Craven was not thought to be a heavy fall-out area; at any rate we were not told so. It was only six or nine months later that it was revealed that Craven had been a fall-out black spot and that Whitehall had kept it quiet. It was a repetition, admittedly on a smaller scale, of the cover-up after the Windscale nuclear accident in 1957 (see page 336). This confirms me in my view, set out in the introduction to *An Englishman Abroad*, that the damage done out of conviction by self-confessed traitors like Burgess and Blunt does not compare with the far greater injuries done to this country by politicians and higher civil servants out of cowardice, self-advancement and a need to save their own skins. The last sixteen years has seen a good deal of that.

I was both surprised and gratified by the success of this book when it was first published in October 1994 though there were, of course, drawbacks. It is standard form nowadays that, bringing out a book, one has to go on a promotional tour. That autumn I was escorted round a good many bookshops in the provinces signing copies of *Writing Home*, these public signing sessions invariably followed by an even longer stint doing what is called 'signing stock'. One was seldom allowed to sign stock in the shop, presumably because the public would be outraged at the speed and indifference with which one did it. Instead I was taken into a back room where, unfeeling and unobserved, I could polish off four hundred copies an hour.

Waterstone's don't seem to have many back rooms so I usually ended up signing stock in the staff room. Bath, Cambridge, Manchester, Leeds . . . these staff rooms are the same: one goes in and there is a nylon shirt hanging up to dry, some socks over the radiator, half a pizza three days old and a bicycle wheel.

I was following round the Australian novelist Peter Carey. He was more Calvinist in his approach than I was, so when fans asked him if he would sign their book 'To Mum and Dad' he refused on the semantically quite proper grounds that they weren't *his* Mum and Dad. Lacking his Antipodean grit I put down whatever the purchasers wanted; since they'd paid £17.50 I felt they were entitled to it.

Still, readers do ask one to write some very peculiar things in their books. One youth said, 'Could you put "To Christine. I'm sorry about last night and it won't happen again!"' This I dutifully did and then had to sign it 'Alan Bennett'. If I'm ever deemed worthy of a biography I'd like to see what Andrew Motion or Humphrey Carpenter will make of that.

Alan Bennett

Past and Present

The Treachery of Books

'What you want to be', Mam said to my brother and me, 'is
gentlemen farmers. They earn up to £10 a week.' This was in
Leeds some time in the early years of the war, when my father, a
butcher at Armley Lodge Road Co-op, was getting £6 a week
and they thought themselves not badly off. So it's not the
modesty of my mother's aspirations that seems surprising now
but the direction. Why gentlemen farmers? And the answer, of
course, was books.

We had, it's true, had some experience of a farm. I was five
when the war started, and Monday 4 September 1939 should
have been my first day at school; but that was not to be. I wish I
could record our family as gathered anxiously round the wireless, as most were at eleven o'clock that Sunday morning, but I
already knew at the age of five that I belonged to a family that
without being in the least bit remarkable or eccentric yet
managed never to be quite like other families. If we had been,
my brother and I would have been evacuated with all the other
children the week before, but Mam and Dad hadn't been able to
face it. So, not quite partaking in the national mood and, as ever,
unbrushed by the wings of history, Mr Chamberlain's broadcast
found us on a tram going down Tong Road into Leeds. Fearing
the worst, my parents had told my brother and me that we were
all going out into the country that day and we were to have a
picnic – something I had hitherto only come across in books. So

3

on that fateful Sunday morning what was occupying my mind was the imminent conjunction of life with literature; that I should remember nothing of the most momentous event in the twentieth century because of the prospect of an experience found in books was, I see now, a melancholy portent.

Nor was the lesson that life was not going to live up to literature slow in coming, since the much-longed-for picnic wasn't eaten as picnics were in books, on a snowy tablecloth set in a field by a stream, but was taken on a form in the bus station at Vicar Lane, where we waited half that day for any bus that would take us out of the supposedly doomed city.

Early that afternoon a bus came, bound for Pateley Bridge, the other side of Harrogate. Somewhere along the way and quite at random the four of us got off and our small odyssey was ended. It was a village called Wilsill, in Nidderdale. There were a few houses, a shop, a school and a church and, though we were miles from any town, even here the stream had been dammed to make a static water tank in readiness for the firefighters and the expected bombs. Opposite the bus-stop was a farm. My father was a shy man and, though I'm sure there were many larger acts of bravery being done elsewhere that day, to knock at the door of the farm and ask some unknown people to take us in still seems to me to be heroic. Their name was Weatherhead and they did take us in and without question, as people were being taken in all over England that first week of the war.

That night Dad took the bus back to Leeds, my mother weeping as if he were returning to the front, and there at Wilsill we stayed – but for how long? My brother, then aged eight, says it was three weeks; to me, three years younger, it seemed months; but, weeks or months, very happy it was until, once it became plain nothing was going to happen for a while, we went back home, leaving Byril Farm (which is now, alas, not a farm and has carriage lamps) standing out in my mind as the one

4

episode in my childhood that lived up to the story-books.

I had read quite a few story-books by this time, as I had learned to read quite early by dint, it seemed to me, of staring over my brother's shoulder at the comic he was reading until suddenly it made sense. Though I liked reading (and showed off at it), it was soon borne in upon me that the world of books was only distantly related to the world in which I lived. The families I read about were not like our family (no family ever quite was). These families had dogs and gardens and lived in country towns equipped with thatched cottages and mill-streams, where the children had adventures, saved lives, caught villains, and found treasure before coming home, tired but happy, to eat sumptuous teas off chequered tablecloths in low-beamed parlours presided over by comfortable pipe-smoking fathers and gentle aproned mothers, who were invariably referred to as Mummy and Daddy.

In an effort to bring this fabulous world closer to my own, more threadbare, existence, I tried as a first step substituting 'Mummy' and 'Daddy' for my usual 'Mam' and 'Dad', but was pretty sharply discouraged. My father was hot on anything smacking of social pretension; there had even been an argument at the font because my aunties had wanted my brother given two Christian names instead of plain one.

Had it been only stories that didn't measure up to the world it wouldn't have been so bad. But it wasn't only fiction that was fiction. Fact too was fiction, as textbooks seemed to bear no more relation to the real world than did the story-books. At school or in my *Boy's Book of the Universe* I read of the minor wonders of nature – the sticklebacks that haunted the most ordinary pond, the newts and toads said to lurk under every stone, and the dragonflies that flitted over the dappled surface. Not, so far as I could see, in Leeds. There were owls in hollow trees, so the nature books said, but I saw no owls – and hollow

5

trees were in pretty short supply too. The only department where nature actually lined up with the text was frog-spawn. Even in Leeds there was that, jamjars of which I duly fetched home to stand beside great wilting bunches of bluebells on the backyard window-sill. But the tadpoles never seemed to graduate to the full-blown frogs the literature predicted, invariably giving up the ghost as soon as they reached the two-legged stage when, unbeknownst to Mam, they would have to be flushed secretly down the lav.

It was the same when we went on holiday. If the books were to be believed, every seashore was littered with starfish and delicately whorled shells, seahorses in every rockpool and crabs the like of which I had seen only in Macfisheries' window. Certainly I never came across them at Morecambe, nor any of the other advertised treasures of the seashore. There was only a vast, untenanted stretch of mud and somewhere beyond it the sea, invisible, unpaddleable and strewn with rolls of barbed wire to discourage any parachutist undiscerning enough to choose to land there.

These evidences of war and the general shortage of treats and toys made me somehow blame the shortcomings of the natural world on the current hostilities. I don't recall seeing a magnolia tree in blossom until I was fifteen or so, and when I did I found myself thinking 'Well, they probably didn't have them during the war.' And so it was with shells and starfish and all the rest of Nature's delights: she had put these small treasures into storage for the duration, along with signposts, neon lights and the slot machines for Five Boys chocolate that stood, invariably empty, on every railway platform.

This sense of deprivation, fully developed by the time I was seven or eight, sometimes came down to particular words. I had read in many stories, beginning I suppose with *Babes in the Wood*, how the childish hero and heroine, lost in the forest, had

6

nevertheless spent a cosy night bedded down on *pine needles*. I had never come across these delightfully accommodating features and wondered where they were to be found. Could one come across them in Leeds? It was not short of parks after all – Gott's Park, Roundhay Park – surely one of them would have pine needles.

And then there was *sward*, a word that was always cropping up in *Robin Hood*. It was what tournaments and duels were invariably fought on. But what was sward? 'Grass,' said my teacher, Miss Timpson, shortly; but I knew it couldn't be. Grass was the wiry, sooty stuff that covered the Rec in Moorfield Road where we played at night after school. That was not sward. So once, hearing of some woods in Bramley, a few miles from where we lived, I went off on the trail of sward, maybe hoping to come across pine needles in the process. I trailed out past the rhubarb fields at Hill Top, over Stanningley Road then down into the valley that runs up from Kirkstall Abbey. But all I found were the same mouldy old trees and stringy grass that we had at Armley. Pine needles, sward, starfish and sticklebacks – they were what you read about in books.

Books are where the gentlemen farmers must have come from too, from Winifred Holtby's *South Riding* perhaps, or something by Phyllis Bentley, both novelists my mother favoured – local celebrities (as much later was John Braine), writers who had escaped the mill or the mine and made good, the making good invariably taking the form of going Down South. These books, and those my brother and I read, would be borrowed from Armley Library at the bottom of Wesley Road, a grand turn-of-the-century building with a marble staircase and stained-glass swing doors.

The Junior Library was in a room of its own, and an institution more intended to discourage children from reading could not have been designed. It was presided over by a fierce

British Legion commissionaire, a relic of the Boer War, who, with his medals and walrus moustache was the image of Hindenburg as pictured on the German stamps in my brother's album. The books were uniformly bound in stout black or maroon covers, so whether they were Henty, Captain Marryat or (my favourite) Hugh Lofting, they looked a pretty unenticing read.

In contrast the Adults' Library was a bright and cheerful place, where Dad would be looking for something funny by Stephen Leacock or what he called 'a good tale', and Mam would be in Non-Fiction seeking her particular brand of genteel escape – sagas of couples who had thrown up everything to start a smallholding (gentlemen farmers in the making) or women like Monica Dickens who had struck out on their own. A particular favourite was William Holt, whose *I Haven't Unpacked* was one of the few books Mam ever bought, and again it was escape – the story of someone brought up, as she had been, in a mill town but who had bought a horse and gone off on his travels.

This theme of escape, very strong in Wells and Priestley, tantalized my parents for much of their lives. Dreams of leaving I suppose they had, and I now share them, feeling myself as nailed to my table as ever my Dad was to his shop counter. They never did escape quite, though they made a shot at it just once when, towards the end of the war, my father gave up his job at the Co-op, answered an advert in the *Meat Trades Journal* and got a job working for a private butcher in Guildford. And in Guildford for a year we lived. Down South. And there were thatched cottages and mill-streams and children who called their parents 'Mummy' and 'Daddy' – the world I had read about in my books, and the world Mam and Dad had read about in theirs.

But, thatched cottages or no thatched cottages, they were not happy, and one miserable December night in 1945 the four of us got off the train at Holbeck and trailed disconsolately back to my grandma's house and reality. It was another lesson that you should not believe what you read in books.

From time to time after this my mother's hands would be covered in terrible eczema, the joints cracked open, the skin scaling away. 'My hands have broken out again,' she would say, and put it down to the wrong soap. But it was as if she was now caged in and this the only 'breaking out' she was capable of.

The few books we owned were largely reference books, bought by subscription through magazines: *Enquire Within, What Everybody Wants to Know* and, with its illustrations of a specimen man and woman (minus private parts and pubic hair), *Everybody's Home Doctor*. No book, whether from the library or otherwise, was ever on view. Anthony Powell's 'Books do furnish a room' was not my mother's way of thinking. 'Books untidy a room' more like, or, as she would have said, 'Books upset.' So if there were any books being read they would be kept out of sight, generally in the cabinet that had once held a wind-up gramophone, bought when they were first married and setting up house.

This undercover attitude to books persisted long after I had grown up and had accumulated books of my own. I worked in the spare room, though it was never dignified as such and just known as the junk room. That was where the books were kept now, and there among the broken lampshades and bits of old carpet and hemmed in by the sewing-machine and the family suitcases I would set up a table and work. To begin with it was for my degree, then it was research in medieval history, and finally writing proper. But to my mother it was all the same: to her my life had not changed since I was fourteen and doing School Certificate, so degree, research or writing plays was always called 'your swotting'.

As a young man my father had some literary ambitions, going in for competitions in magazines such as *Tit-Bits* and even sending in little paragraphs and being paid. By the forties his efforts were concentrated on one competition, Bullets, a feature of the magazine *John Bull*, the point of which was to come up with a telling phrase on a given topic, the phrase to be witty, ironic or ambiguous – in effect a verbal cartoon. Once he had regularly won small prizes, but though he went on plugging away during the war, and until the magazine folded in the late forties, he won only a few pounds.

I couldn't get the hang of Bullets or see the point or the humour of the entries that won; they seemed like Tommy Handley's jokes – everybody said they were funny, but they never made you laugh. If I missed *John Bull* when it closed down it was for its cover paintings, in particular the landscapes of Rowland Hilder – idyllic downland farms, beech trees against a winter sky – or the townscapes of deaf and dumb artist A. R. Thomson, as English as Norman Rockwell was American.

In later life my father was often ill and this started him reading again, only now his taste was much more eclectic and he would try any book he found on my shelves. Knowing nothing of reputation and just judging a book by whether he could 'get into it' or not, he lapped up Evelyn Waugh and Graham Greene, revelled in Nancy Mitford, but couldn't take (at opposite extremes) Buchan or E. F. Benson; Orwell he just about managed ('though there's not much of a tale to it'), and he liked Gavin Maxwell and especially Wilfred Thesiger. When he came to the episode in *Ring of Bright Water* where a Scots road-mender casually kills one of Maxwell's pet otters with a spade he burst out, 'Why, the bad sod!'

This phrase had a literary history and was something of a family joke. As a child Dad had been taken to the Grand Theatre to see *Uncle Tom's Cabin* and in the scene in which Uncle Tom was being flogged by the overseer, Simon Legree, a woman sitting next to Dad in the gallery shouted out, 'You bad sod!' The actor playing Simon Legree stopped, looked up at the gallery, leered, and then laid it on twice as hard.

Towards the end of his life I had so taken it for granted that our taste in reading coincided that I forgot how shy and fastidious my father was and how far his world still was from mine. Though there may have been a priggish element of 'I think you are now ready for this' about it, I did think that when I gave him Philip Roth's *Portnoy's Complaint* he would find it as funny as I did. Always anxious to talk about what he had read, on my next visit home he never mentioned it, and I later found it back on the shelf, the jacket marking the twenty pages or so that he had got through before deciding it was pornography and not something for him, and by implication not something for me, though nothing was ever said. It was a miscalculation that mortifies me to this day.

My mother was more broadminded and might have found *Portnoy's Complaint* quite funny, but Dad's literary renaissance never infected her, and for years her reading was largely confined to *Woman's Own* and in particular to the column written by Beverley Nichols, of whom she was a great fan. But seeing the Brontës frequently referred to in the *Yorkshire Evening Post* she began to persuade herself she had read them or perhaps would like to – maybe because (another escape story) if they hadn't got away from their surroundings they had at any rate transcended them. So on a bleak February day in the late forties she and I took the Keighley bus to Haworth to see the famous parsonage. Not so famous then, Haworth was still happily unaware of its potential as a tourist trap, its situation on the frontiers of *Last of the Summer Wine* country far in the future. The place must have had some charm, but it looked to me like any other grim mill town and all I could think as we toiled up that long hill was that it must be even more dismal on a Sunday.

We were the only visitors to the parsonage that day, and it was as dark and damp as it must have been when the famous trio lived there. Ramshackle and unrenovated, it was, even for 1948, a decidedly eccentric museum, looked after by a lady who, if not actually a contemporary of the Brontës, seemed their sister in suffering. Objects around the house were only haphazardly labelled: the sofa on which Emily died, for instance, just had pinned to it a yellowing piece of paper that said starkly, 'Sofa Emily died on'. Mam was horrified. The fireplace wanted blackleading and the curtains were a disgrace. 'Too busy writing their books to keep the place up to scratch,' was her comment.

Though this was long before the tasteful pall of heritage was laid across the past, the parsonage can have survived in this Victorian state only a few years longer. Had it been kept as it was then, it would today be in a museum itself, a museum of museums perhaps. It would certainly be more interesting and characteristic than the branch of Laura Ashley the parsonage is nowadays, though there's not much doubt which Mam would have preferred.

My parents always felt that had they been educated their lives and indeed their characters would have been different. They imagined books would make them less shy and (always an ambition) able to 'mix'. Quiet and never particularly gregarious, they cherished a lifelong longing to 'branch out', with books somehow the key to it. This unsatisfied dream they have bequeathed to me, so that without any conscious intention I find I am often including in plays or films what is essentially the same scene: someone is standing at a bookcase; it may be a boy with no education, not daring to choose a book, or a wife anxious to share in the literary world of men; it can be Joe Orton looking at Kenneth Halliwell's bookcase and despairing of ever catching

up, or even Coral Browne, idly turning over the pages of Guy
Burgess's books while being quizzed about Cyril Connolly,
whom she does not know. One way or another they are all
standing in for my parents and sharing their uncertainty about
books. As for me, while I'm not baffled by books, I can't see how
anyone can love them ('He loved books'). I can't see how anyone
can 'love literature'. What does that mean? Of course, one
advantage of being a gentleman farmer is that you seldom have
to grapple with such questions.

Leeds Trams

There was a point during the Second World War when my father took up the double bass. To recall the trams of my boyhood is to be reminded particularly of that time.

It is around 1942 and we are living in the house my parents bought when they got married, 12 Halliday Place in Upper Armley. The Hallidays are handily situated for two tram routes, and if we are going into town, rather than to Grandma's in Wortley, the quickest way is to take a number 14. This means a walk across Ridge Road, down past the back of Christ Church (and Miss Marsden's the confectioner's) to Stanningley Road. Stanningley Road is already a dual carriageway because the tram tracks running down the middle of the road are pebbled and enclosed by railings, so splitting what little traffic there is into lanes. The Stanningley trams are generally somewhat superior to those on other routes, more upholstered, and when the more modern streamlined variety comes in after the war, it is more likely to be found on this route than elsewhere. But the drawback with the Stanningley Road trams is that they come down from Bramley or even Rodley, and are always pretty crowded, so more often than not we go for the other route, the number 16, which means walking up Moorfield Road to Charleycake Park and Whingate Junction.

This being the terminus, the tram is empty and as likely as not waiting, or, if we've just missed one, the next will already be in sight, swaying up Whingate. We wait as the driver swings outside and with a great twang hauls over the bogey ready for the journey back, while upstairs the conductor strolls down the aisle, reversing the seats before winding back the indicator on the front. The driver and conductor then get off and have their break sat on the form by the tram-stop, the driver generally older and more solid than the conductor (or, I suppose, the conductress, though I don't recall conductresses coming in until after the war).

Dad is a smoker, so we troop upstairs rather than going 'inside', the word a reminder of the time when upstairs was also outside. On some trams in 1942 it still is, because in these early years of the war a few open-ended trams have been brought back into service. We wedge ourselves in the front corner to be exposed to the wind and weather, an unexpected treat, and also an antidote to the travel sickness from which both my brother and I suffer, though I realize now that this must have been due as much to all the smoking that went on as to the motion of the tram itself. Neither of us ever actually is sick, but it's not uncommon and somewhere on the tram is a bin of sand just in case.

So the four of us – Mam, Dad, my brother and me – are ensconced on the tram sailing down Tong Road into town or, if we are going to see Grandma, who lives in the Gilpins, we will get off halfway at Fourteenth Avenue.

Around 1942, though, we come into the double-bass period, when some of our tram journeys become fraught with embarrassment. Dad is a good amateur violinist, largely self-taught, so taking up the double bass isn't such a big step. He practises in the front room, which is never used for anything else, and, I suppose because the bass never has the tune, it sounds terrible; he sounds as if he's sawing (which he also does, actually, as one of his other hobbies is fretwork). Though the instrument is large the repertoire is small, except in one area: swing. Until now Dad has never had much time for swing, or popular music generally; his idea of a good time is to turn on the Home Service and play along with the hymns on *Sunday Half Hour*, or (more tentatively) with the light classics that are the staple of Albert Sandler and his Palm Court Orchestra. But now, with Dad in the grip of this new craze, Mam, my brother and I are made to gather round the wireless, tuned these days to the Light Programme, so that we can listen to dance-band music.

'Listen, Mam. Do you hear the beat? That's the bass. That'll be me.'

Dad has joined a part-time dance band. Even at eight years old I know that this is not a very good idea and just another of his crazes (the fretwork, the home-made beer) – schemes Dad has thought up to make a bit of money. So now we are walking up Moorfield Road to get the tram again, only this time to go and watch Dad play in his band somewhere in Wortley, and our carefree family of four has been joined by a fifth, a huge and threatening cuckoo, the double bass.

Knowing what is to happen, the family make no attempt to go upstairs, but scuttle inside while Dad begins to negotiate with the conductor. The conductor spends a lot of his time in the little cubby-hole under the winding metal stairs. There's often a radiator here that he perches on, and it's also where the bell-pull hangs, in those days untouchable by passengers, though it's often no fancier than a knotted leather thong. In his cubby-hole the conductor keeps a tin box with his spare tickets and other impedimenta which at the end of the journey he will carry down to the other end of the tram. The niche that protects the conductor from the passengers is also just about big enough to protect the double bass, but when Dad suggests this there is invariably an argument, which he never wins, the clincher generally coming when the conductor points out that strictly speaking 'that thing' isn't allowed on the tram at all. So while we sit inside and pretend he isn't with us, Dad stands on the platform grasping the bass by the neck as if he's about to give a solo. He gets in the way of the conductor, he gets in the way of the people getting on and off, and, always a mild man, it must have been more embarrassing for him than it ever was for us.

Happily this dance-band phase, like the fretwork and the herb beer, doesn't last long. He gets bored with the fretwork, the herb beer regularly explodes in the larder, and the double bass is eventually advertised in the Miscellaneous column of the *Evening Post* and we can go back to sitting on the top deck again.

After the war we move to Far Headingley, where Dad, having worked all his life for the Co-op, now has a shop of his own just below the tram-sheds opposite St Chad's. We live over the shop, so I sleep and wake to the sound of trams: trams getting up speed for the hill before Weetwood Lane, trams spinning down from West Park, trams shunted around in the sheds in the middle of the night, the scraping of wheels, the clanging of the bell.

It is not just the passage of time that makes me invest the trams of those days with such pleasure. To be on a tram sailing down Headingley Lane on a fine evening lifted the heart at the time just as it does in memory. I went to school by tram, the fare a halfpenny from St Chad's to the Ring Road. A group of us at the Modern School scorned school dinners and came home for lunch, catching the tram from another terminus at West Park. We were all keen on music and went every Saturday to hear the Yorkshire Symphony Orchestra in the Town Hall, and it was on a tram at West Park that another sixth-former, 'Fanny' Fielder, sang to me the opening bars of Brahms's Second Piano Concerto, which I'd never heard and which the YSO was playing that coming Saturday. Trams came into that too, because after the concert many of the musicians went home by tram (though none with a double bass), sitting there, rather shabby and ordinary and often with tab ends in their mouths, worlds away from the Delius, Walton and Brahms which they had been playing. It was a first lesson to me that art doesn't have much to do with appearances, and that ordinary middle-aged men in raincoats can be instruments of the sublime.

Odd details about trams come back to me now, like the slatted platforms, brown with dust, that were slung underneath either end, like some urban cowcatcher; or the little niche in the glass of the window on the seat facing the top of the stairs so that you could slide it open and hang out; and how convivial trams were, the seats reversible so that if you chose you could make up a four whenever you wanted.

How they work was always a mystery. As a child I had difficulty in understanding that the turning motion the driver made with the handle was what drove the tram, it seeming more like mixing than driving. And then there was the imposing demeanour of the ticket inspectors, invested with a spurious grandeur on a par with the one-armed man who showed you to your seat in Schofield's Café, or the manager of the Cottage Road cinema in his dinner-jacket, or gents' outfitters in general.

I don't recall anyone ever collecting tram numbers, but the route numbers had a certain mystique, the even numbers slightly superior to the odd, which tended to belong to trams going to Gipton, Harehills, or Belle Isle, parts of Leeds where I'd never ventured. And Kirkstall will always be 4, just as Lawnswood is 1.

Buses have never inspired the same affection – too comfortable and cushioned to have a moral dimension. Trams were bare and bony, transport reduced to its basic elements, and they had a song to sing, which buses never did. I was away at university when they started to phase them out, Leeds as always in too much of a hurry to get to the future, and so doing the wrong thing. I knew at the time that it was a mistake, just as Beeching was a mistake, and that life was starting to get nastier. If trams ever come back, though, they should come back not as curiosities, nor, God help us, as part of the heritage, but as a cheap and sensible way of getting from point A to point B, and with a bit of poetry thrown in.

Not History at All . . .

When Brian Harrison invited me to take part in this seminar,* I warned him that I knew little about university theatre and that, a magisterial overview not being forthcoming, the most you were likely to get would be an exercise in licensed name-dropping. Even in that I find I was over-optimistic. I recall few names that became names – the broadcaster Russell Harty, the director Patrick Garland, and then I'm done. It hardly adds up to a generation. So if I confine myself to what is really a memoir of my somewhat atypical career outside university theatre it's not because I believe that this was the most significant thing going on at the time, just that I so seldom ventured out of my college that I didn't have much notion of what was happening outside at all.

The years after the war had seen a great flowering of talent in the theatre in Oxford. The backlog of ex-service under-graduates who came up then included some, like film director John Schlesinger, who were veterans of that ENSA concert party Peter Nichols has written about in *Privates on Parade*. There was sterner stuff in directors in the making like Lindsay Anderson and Ronald Eyre, and even management was represented in the infant impresario Michael Codron. Leading the rout and easily the most colourful figure, in clothes which

* On 'The History of the University since 1945', held at Nuffield College, Oxford, in 1986.

in those days started fights but now would scarcely lift an eyebrow, was Kenneth Tynan. By 1954 these were long gone, but most undergraduates still came up, as I did, after two years' national service.

I imagine the point may have come up in earlier sessions of this seminar, but the abolition of national service later in the fifties must have made an incalculable difference to the university in all sorts of ways. I speak only for myself. Although when I came up I was two years older than most undergraduates are now, and was here in all for some eight years, it took me all that time to hit upon what I wanted to do. I found my niche eventually, but if I'd come here straight from school I should probably still be looking.

My college, Exeter, was in 1954 a fairly modest, not to say undistinguished establishment. Which was precisely why I'd chosen it, as I'd stand a better chance there, I reasoned, than at socially more exalted foundations such as Trinity, which I think was in the same group. My mother had actually suggested I try Balliol. (She mispronounced the name, of course, but I'm not sure I didn't at that time.) My mother's idea of a university owed less to Cardinal Newman than it did to Beverley Nichols, of whose weekly column in the *Woman's Own* she was a great fan. Beverley had been to Balliol, my mother said, so why not me? There were plenty of reasons, the chief one being that it was so academically tip-top. It was also quite ugly. At seventeen I was a bit of an architectural snob. I was coming to Oxford hell-bent on going through a process I suppose I thought of as 'blossoming', and I saw as an essential ingredient in the blossoming process a nice period background. Exeter's strong artistic suit was its connection with Morris and Burne-Jones, but the Pre-Raphaelites weren't quite back in fashion by 1954 so even in this department I thought it no great shakes. Still it did have its picturesque corners, though not enough to attract the more fastidious and discerning applicants, who would, I hoped, be winnowed out by the glories of Magdalen or St John's, thus leaving the field open to dowdy and devious creatures like myself.

One jokes about these options now but they were no joke then, and it all had to be decided at home – the wireless off, the kitchen table cleared and wiped (no more certain way of being rejected, I thought, than jam on the entrance form). In the mystifying permutations of choice my parents stood by helpless; they scarcely knew what a university was, let alone the status of its component parts. The irony, of course, was that when I finally landed up at Exeter I found that in my callow assessment of college form I had not been unique. Others had reasoned in the same way, with the result that Exeter was far harder to get into than anywhere else.

In 1954 Exeter was an inward-looking college. Few of its members figured in the wider life of the university, and it had a close-knit family atmosphere. This should have meant that in-college societies were that much more vigorous, but this certainly wasn't true of drama. So far as I recall, Exeter's dramatic society was in abeyance the whole of my time as an undergraduate. This was no doubt a relief to the college. Dons have always been dubious about drama. Though rowing, and indeed running, can scarcely be said to hone the mind, they have always been looked on more favourably than the stage. Acting is somehow thought to rot both mind and character. Whereas it would be inconceivable to stop someone rowing or running in their final year, it was (and perhaps still is) quite common to forbid him or her to act.

None of which – acting, rowing, or running – bothered me much, as I wasn't inclined to do any of them. I had carried over from national service (and in this I'm sure I wasn't alone) a suspicion of volunteering, of joining, indeed of conspicuous activity of any sort. So I became a member of no clubs; no cards decorated my mantelpiece; no societies met in my rooms. It was all very dull and, apart from the fact that I had to share a set with someone who had been in the same barrack room for much of my national service and whom I loathed and who loathed me, I was quite happy.

In the army one of my friends was Michael Frayn, subsequently the novelist and playwright. He was now at Cambridge, and his attitude was the opposite of mine. In the first week of his first term he was writing for *Varsity*, had enrolled with the Footlights, and had taken to university life with a large, unselfconscious splash. In those days we used to correspond, and whereas my letters accuse him of 'selling out', his letters to me, slightly more sensibly, urge me to pull my socks up. On one point in particular we differed absolutely and this was college life. Whereas I was happy to settle down in the cosy, undemanding atmosphere of the Exeter Junior Common Room, Frayn regarded his college, Emmanuel, as little more than an address – and not a very smart one at that. And since Exeter was to me all that I wanted in the way of a club, this was another reason for not joining any others. There was certainly no thought of joining either OUDS or the Experimental Theatre Club, both somehow sounding wrong: OUDS the plump, self-assured, good-mannered theatre of the Establishment; ETC the opposite – seedy, plaintive, out at the elbows. What there was not, of course, was anything like the Cambridge Footlights, with a tradition of revue and comedy-writing. I'm sure if there had been I would have failed to join that too.

So it was with a certain sense of already having thrown in the towel that I settled down to college life. The JCR in Exeter at that time was more central to the life of the college than in other colleges I visited. At the heart of it was the institution of the Suggestions Book. As a repository of actual suggestions, the

Suggestions Book was useless, but it served besides as a college newspaper, a diary, a forum for discussion, and a space in which those who were so inclined could attempt to amuse and even paddle in the direction of literature. The result was a volume (in time a succession of volumes) that was parochial, silly and obscene, but to me, and possibly to others, of a particular value. A family atmosphere, a captive audience and a set of shared references are good conditions in which to learn to write, and I think it was through my contributions to the JCR Suggestions Book that I first realized I could make people laugh and liked doing it.

At the end of each term the JCR held a smoking-concert. These smokers were really just a dramatized version of the Suggestions Book: vulgar, private, silly – all the things my literary friends abhorred. They were uproarious drunken affairs, confined to members of the college and in the direct line of those camp concerts POWs spent their time acting in when they weren't busy tunnelling under the foundations. One regular feature was a Queen's Christmas Broadcast; very tame it would seem now, but in those pre-satirical days, when HMQ's annual pronouncement was treated with hushed reverence, the very idea of it seemed sacrilegiously funny. And it was for one of these smoking-concerts that I wrote a cod Anglican sermon, something I found no problem doing as I'd sat through so many in my youth. It took me half an hour to put together, and, since it later figured in (indeed earned me my place in) *Beyond the Fringe*, it was undoubtedly the most profitable half-hour I've ever spent. At the same time, having written it I had no sense that a corner had been turned.

I had always been a late starter, so, friendly though the atmosphere was, I didn't pluck up courage to take part even in these JCR smokers until my third year, by which time my days at the university seemed numbered. However, after I'd taken my degree I found myself able to stay on as a postgraduate, doing research on Richard II. I also began to teach a little, first for Magdalen and then for Exeter. I had some sense, I think, that making people laugh was not a proper activity for a post-graduate and that I ought somehow to be acquiring more dignity; except that by now I was being asked to perform in other colleges and do cabaret for dances and Commem Balls, and was sometimes even paid. The situation was more delicate because I was supervised in my research by the medieval historian Bruce McFarlane. McFarlane was a man of great austerity and singleness of mind. He was shy, very kind, and the most impressive teacher, and in some ways the most impressive man, I have ever come across. One could go and chat to him without seemingly ever touching on the subject of one's research and come away convinced that studying one's tiny slip of a subject (mine was Richard II's retinue from 1388 to 1399) was the only thing in the world worth doing. He knew a little of my cabaret performances, but they were never referred to. Around this time I recorded some sketches for BBC radio, and told him when they were due to be broadcast; 'I listened,' was all he ever said.

By this time I had been at Oxford some five years, and it was plain to me, if I did not quite admit it to myself, that I was not going to make a don. To begin with I had no memory to speak of, and the notes of my research proliferated without ever congealing into anything approaching a thesis. As for teaching, I could never find sufficient comments to fill the necessary hour, and nor could my pupils. If I ventured on argument I was soon floored, and the tutorials ended in awkward silence. Eventually I took to putting the clock on before my pupils arrived, so there was less time to fill.

Deliverance came in the summer of 1959. In that year the Oxford Theatre Group first put on a revue on the fringe at the

Edinburgh Festival. Feeling immensely old and foolish at twenty-five, I nervously auditioned for the writer and director Stanley Daniels. He was an American, also a postgraduate, who appeared (so much for my qualms) at least forty, with no dignity at all nor seeming to want any. I see his name nowadays in the credits as one of the producers of the excellent American TV series *Taxi*. We performed at the Cranston Street Hall in Edinburgh, where in the same hall the previous year the Oxford Theatre Group had premièred Willis Hall's *The Long, the Short and the Tall* and where another première a few years later was Tom Stoppard's *Rosencrantz and Guildenstern are Dead*. In any account of university theatre the OTG should figure largely. Our contribution in 1959 was called *Better Late*. It was a great success, to the extent that the official Festival took note and the following year decided to put on a revue of its own, inviting Peter Cook and Jonathan Miller from Cambridge and Dudley Moore and myself from Oxford to write and perform it. This we did firstly in Edinburgh in 1960 and subsequently in the West End. Though Dudley had been an organ scholar at Magdalen and we had even appeared on the same bill, I don't think we had ever met until the first script conference for *Beyond the Fringe*.

While I was writing this I was puzzled why, when I'd performed so little at university and not been an avid playgoer, I yet remembered Oxford as a place of theatrical excitement. I think it was that I somehow regarded the nightly experience of dining in hall as a kind of theatre, a theatre in which the undergraduates were the audience and the actors were the dons. At Exeter they entered – *climbed* almost – on to the stage from the mysterious backstage of the Senior Common Room, a room dimly remembered from one's scholarship interview and not seen again until three years later, when one entered it before one's Schools Dinner. Fanciful perhaps to compare the bang of the block for grace with the knocks that signal the rise of the curtain at the Comédie-Française, but there was, as there is in every college, a regular repertory company enlivened at week-ends and on guest nights by visitors and the occasional star. Auden I remember seeing once, hearing that quacking voice without recognizing the face, which in the mid-fifties had just begun to go under the harrow. Richard Burton was there one night, Dennis Healey, Harold Wilson – hardly fabled names but still names one had read in the papers, creatures from a world elsewhere. Nowadays dining arrangements at Exeter are different. The undergraduates are halfway through their meal when High Table comes in, so they don't have this sense of a nightly performance that I had – and feel it faintly ridiculous to have had.

When I moved to Magdalen, as the most junior of junior lecturers, it was rather different. Whereas Exeter was still in the era of the proscenium arch with the dons entering stage left in single file, at Magdalen it was altogether more dramatic and the choreography more fluid. There the fellows made a swift dash around the cloisters before entering in a crowd through the body of the hall, streaming through the standing assembly and up to High Table as if directed by Ariane Mnouchkine or some fashionable young man from the RSC. At Magdalen too the visitors were grander and the regular repertory company more distinguished: C. S. Lewis, Gilbert Ryle, A. J. P. Taylor, daunting neighbours at dinner, my memories of those meals as vivid and painful as any embarrassment that happened to me subsequently on the stage. The first or second time I dined there I sat down and, as I pushed in my chair, caught the sleeves of my BA gown under the legs. Despite the fact that my movements were thus severely restricted I was too shy to get up and free them. It was a particularly delicious dinner that night, but I saw little of it. The scouts kept lowering dishes towards me but hovered tantalizingly out of reach of my pinioned arms. As I thus appeared to wave away dish after dish my neighbour leaned over solicitously and said, 'You know, if you're a vegetarian, they'll do you something special.'

Much of the time I was at Magdalen I was playing in *Beyond The Fringe* in London and commuting to Oxford three days a week in order to teach. Or not to teach, because I wasn't getting any better at it, though the celebrity of the revue to some degree compensated my pupils for the shortcomings of the tuition. This period came to an end in 1962, when the show went to Broadway, thus putting an end to my dwindling hopes of being a historian. The rest, one might say pompously, is history. Except that in my case the opposite was true. What it had been was history. What it was to be was not history at all.

Uncle Clarence

Once we have located the cemetery, the grave itself is not hard to find, one of a row of headstones just inside the gate and backing on to a railway. Flanders in April and it is, not inappropriately, raining, clogging our shoes the famous mud. The stone gives the date of his death, 21 October 1917, but not his age. He was twenty.

He was always twenty all through my childhood, because of the photograph on the piano at my grandmother's house in Leeds. He was her only son. He sits in his uniform and puttees in Mr Lonnergan's studio down Woodsley Road. Lonnergan's, a classy place that does you a good likeness. Less classy but still doing a good likeness, Mr Lonnergan takes pictures of my brother and me in 1944 in the closing stages of the next war. An artier study this, two boys aged twelve and nine emerge from a shadowy background to look unsmiling at Mr Lonnergan under his cloth. My brother is in his Morley Grammar School blazer, his hand resting unselfconsciously on my grey-flannelled shoulder. In his picture Uncle Clarence is on embarkation leave from the King's Royal Rifles. In 1944 we too are going away, though not to certain death, only 'Down South' to fulfil a dream of my father's. He has answered an advert in the *Meat Trades Journal* and, having worked twenty-five years for the Co-op, is now going to manage a family butcher's in Guildford. Uncle Clarence never comes back but we are back within the

29

year, his photograph still standing on the piano on its lace doily, and now ours has been put beside it.

The piano itself does not belong to Grandma. She gives it house room at 7 Gilpin Place for her sister-in-law, Aunt Eveline. Aunt Eveline has never married and has beautiful handwriting. Her name is on all the music in the piano stool, and in her time she accompanied the silent films at the Electric Cinema, Bradford. Come the talkies, she turns housekeeper and now looks after a Mr Wilson, sometime chairman of the Bradford Dyers' Association, who is a widower with a fancy woman, whom Aunt Eveline dislikes because she has dyed hair and is not Aunt Eveline. On Sundays there are musical evenings in the front room at Gilpin Place. The children are warned to keep back as a shovelful of burning coals from the kitchen range is carried smoking through the house to light the fire in the sitting-room before we sit down to high tea in the kitchen. After tea, the sitting-room still smelling of smoke, Aunt Eveline arranges herself on the piano stool and with my father on the violin ('Now then, Walter, what shall we give them?') kicks off with a selection from *Glamorous Night*. Then, having played themselves in, they accompany Uncle George, my father's brother, in some songs. Uncle George is a bricklayer and has a fine voice and a face as red as his bricks. He sings 'Bless This House' and 'Where'er You Walk', and sometimes Grandma has a little cry. These occasions go on until about 1950, when Grandma dies.

Grandma, whose name is Mary Ann Peel, has three daughters, Kathleen, Lemira and my mother, Lilian. Clarence is the eldest child, and the only son. Whenever he is talked of it is always 'Our Clarence' or, to my brother and me, 'Your Uncle Clarence'. But he is only our would-be uncle, an uncle-who-might-have-been, not like my father's brothers, uncles of flesh and blood, two of them veterans of the same war and very much alive. We are his nephews by prolepsis and he our posthumous uncle, protected even in death by the convention that children do not refer to relatives by anything so naked as their name.

When Uncle Clarence's name comes up it is generally in connection with the undisputed nobility of his character. What is disputed is which of the sisters resembles him most. It is accepted in our wing of the family that this role belongs to my mother, who certainly looks most like him. The prettiest of the three, she marries early and does not get on with the other two, who marry late. Clarence, later to become a silly-ass kind of name, a name out of farce and, like Albert, never revamped, remains in our family the name of a saint. If my mother is asked about Uncle Clarence the reply is always 'He was a love. He was a grand fellow.' What job he did in the few years given to him to have a job, whether he had a dog or a bike or a girlfriend, none of this I know or bother to ask, and with both my aunties dead there is no one now who does know. My mother lives, but she does not remember she had a brother, or even what 'a brother' is. When asked, she still says, 'He was a grand fellow.' She says the same now about my father. I am a grand fellow too. In these her flat, unmemoried days she would probably say the same about Adolf Hitler.

In the front room at Gilpin Place is an elaborate dresser, with mirrors and alcoves and fretwork shelves. Stripped of its warm chestnut varnish, it will have gone up in the world now, moved from Leeds 12 to Leeds 16 to grace the modish kitchen of a polytechnic lecturer or a designer at Yorkshire TV. In my time this dresser is laden with ornaments housing Grandma's hoard of silver paper, and the drawers are stuffed with bundles of seaside postcards: Sunset across the Bay, Morecambe; The Illuminations, Blackpool; The Bandstand, Lytham St Annes. Glossy, deckle-edged cards in rich purples and browns. To my brother and me, who have never seen fairy lights along the prom or the sands without tank traps and barbed wire, they are what the world was like Before the War. We take the cards and steam off any Edward VII or George V stamps to use as (pretty mediocre) swaps. Among the picture postcards are photographs on stiffer card: Grandma on outings with the ladies' bowling club, striding along some promenade in a long, laughing line, big ladies in cloche hats and black duster coats on trips to Bangor or Dunoon.

The cupboard in the dresser has more mysterious artefacts: old scent sprays, cigar-cutters, some candle-snuffers and a pile of ten-inch 78s in torn brown-paper covers. One is 'I Lift up My Finger and I Say Tweet Tweet, Hush Hush, Now Now, Come Come'. I find some needles in the cupboard and play it on the wind-up gramophone in its red Rexine cover. In theory the dresser is out of bounds and I can only look in it if my brother is out playing with his pals or swimming at Armley Baths and Grandma and I are alone in the house. This is generally on a Saturday afternoon. She dozes in front of the kitchen fire while I investigate the cupboard in the front room. 'Rooting' she calls it. From time to time she wakes up. 'What are you doing in there?' I say nothing. 'Are you rooting? Give over.'

In the first year of the war there is a tin of biscuits in the dresser. The biscuits have long since gone but the legend of them remains, and I always think if I can get to the very back of the cupboard there will be another tin that has been forgotten. There are plenty of other tins. When I ask what's in them my grandmother always gives the same answer: 'Chums.' It is a joke which never fails to amuse her. But before I know that chums are friends they are something mysterious, sweet and secret, that one should not look for because forbidden.

Whereas the kitchen cupboard is dedicated to use, with the old familiar cutlery, threadbare tablecloths, and knives that years of sharpening have brought to the width of skewers, the front-room cupboard houses stuff that never gets used, often in sets: the set of trifle glasses with the green stems, the set of cake knives won at a whist drive, besides all the items no well-run household should be without (grapefruit knives, a cheese-slice) but which are never actually required. It is a museum, this cupboard, to a theory of domestic economy. But it is also a shrine. For somewhere among the packets of doilies and cake frills, the EPNS salad-servers, the packets of spills in violent colours, the whist scoring-cards and the enema in its black box, somewhere among all this is the box with Uncle Clarence's Victory medal, 'which', the citation says, 'would have been conferred on C7/044 Pte C. E. Peel, had he lived'. The letter is dated Winchester, 10 May 1921. 'In forwarding the Decoration I am commanded by the King to assure you of His Majesty's high appreciation of the services rendered.' Even as a small child rooting for biscuits, I can see that His Majesty's high appreciation didn't amount to much.

Besides, what His Majesty's high appreciation didn't run to – could not be expected to run to – was that Uncle Clarence had been ruptured. So, while everyone who died in this war died needlessly, Uncle Clarence died more needlessly than most. My mother always says he should not have gone at all. I do not quite know what 'being ruptured' means. Some shame attaches to it, I know, because Mr Dixon, who takes Standard 5 at Armley National, where I go to school, is ruptured and all the boys think it is a joke. Mr Dixon is the first male teacher I have come up against. He is short and fat and said to wear a truss. What a truss is I don't know either, but I think of it as a device to stop your balls popping out. I find it difficult to connect – still less reconcile – someone as noble as Uncle Clarence and a condition that is both shameful and comical and affects such as Mr Dixon, and maybe I pity Uncle Clarence less for his early death than for his earlier rupture. Though, as my mother says, the one should have prevented the other, because in that condition he could not enlist. With the risk attaching to any surgical operation at that time, he was under no obligation to have the rupture treated, so for a year or two the matter was left and he went on living at home with his sisters. But in the third year of the war he found himself jeered at in the street, taunted by girls from the munitions works, and so he went into St James's, had the operation, and in due course joined up. And here he sits in the photograph, just three months before his death, a whole man again.

In the photograph he is wearing puttees. At what point private soldiers ceased to wear these long bandages wrapped round their legs I don't know. It is certainly gaiters by 1939, 'anklets webbing khaki, pairs two' when I am called up in 1952. But the puttee survives (along with many of the attitudes that go with it) in that stagnant military backwater the Army Cadet Corps. No school I ever attend runs to one, but in the short time we are in Guildford my brother is a pupil at the grammar school there and in a uniform identical to that of Uncle Clarence goes on manoeuvres at Pirbright. I watch him as he winds off these muddy brown bandages to find his legs ridged like those of the common house fly, pictured one thousand times life-size in the *Children's Encyclopedia*.

I never remember anyone mentioning Uncle Clarence's grave. There is no photograph of that in the dresser, only a picture of the war-memorial tablet in St Mary of Bethany, Tong Road. If he has a grave, no one visits it. My grandmother never goes abroad, nor do my parents for that matter, and, though they think of themselves as women of the world, Aunty Kathleen and Aunty Myra only take to globe-trotting late in life. So, knowing only that he had died at Ypres in 1917, in March 1986 I write to the War Graves Commission at Maidenhead, curious to know if he is just a name on a monument or whether he enjoys the luxury of a burial place. It turns out to be more than one and less than the other. For the records say that, though he is commemorated by a special memorial in Larchwood (Railway Cuttings) Cemetery and is thought to lie within that cemetery, the exact location of his body is lost. So now it is a wet Friday morning and we have come over on the hovercraft and are driving through Saint-Omer and north to Zillebeke, a village south-east of Ypres, or since we have now crossed the Belgian frontier, Ieper.

The guidebook says there were three battles at Ypres. The first, in 1914, ended in stalemate and marked the beginning of trench warfare. The second, in 1915, saw the first use of gas. The *Blue Guide* calls 'Passchendaele', the third battle, in 1917, 'tragic and barren', as if that distinguished it from the previous two. The ground gained or lost in each case amounted to a few kilometres. The dead, not noted in the *Blue Guide*, amounted to a quarter of a million.

So now the cemeteries are everywhere, some one hundred and seventy in this salient alone, neat and regular, with their gates and walls and entrances like Roman camps, much neater and more orderly than the suburbs and factory farms they now find themselves among, as if the dead are here to garrison the living, with the countryside not caring, though the place-names aren't hazed over at all, and each location is immaculately signposted. The cemeteries are so thick on the ground that we can't find Larchwood and eventually end up down a cul-de-sac at Hill 60, the slight vantage point south of the town that changed hands many times during the fighting. Now it's a bare, muddy common with a stone telling its history and a memorial to the dead left entombed in its burrows. There is a car park and a home-made museum-cum-café with vases made out of shell cases and a pin-table. Bungalows back on to the common, with garden sheds. One has a car-port and a Peugeot in the drive.

Rustic wooden seats denote this desolate place a picnic area, though nothing much grows, grass the permanent casualty, the ground as brown and bare as an end-of-the-season goalmouth. Was it for this the clay grew tall, for the plastic flowers in the picture windows, the fishman with his van, and a boy riding over the ancient humps of trenches on his BMX bike? Well, yes, I suppose it was.

Unable still to find our cemetery, we give it up and drive back into Ypres and eat a waffle in a chocolate shop, where plump businessmen dally with the proprietress while choosing pralines for the weekend. They go back to the office, tiny boxes of chocolates dangling from one finger, while we drive out on the Menin Road in the rain. Eventually we spot the tip of a cross across a sloping field. There is a railway and there are trees which may be larches and here is the signpost, broken off by a tractor and lying in the ditch.

The cemetery is over a crossing on the far side of a single-track railway. There is a gate, a long finger of lawn alongside the railway, another gate and the burial-ground proper: Uncle Clarence's stone, the stone which is not his grave, is in a row backing on to the railway.

Known to be buried in this cemetery
C7/044
Rifleman C. E. Peel.
King's Royal Rifle Corps.
21 October 1917
†
Their Glory Shall not be Blotted Out.

To one side is a Gunner Hucklesby of the Royal Field Artillery, to the other a Private Oliver of the Hampshires. It is like seeing who is in the next bed in a barrack room. Many of the